The Thirties
for Keyboard

Music arranged and processed by Barnes Music Engraving Ltd
East Sussex TN22 4HA, UK

Cover design by xheight Limited

Published 1995

All Of Me

Words and Music by Seymour Simons and Gerald Marks

Suggested Registration: Jazz Guitar
Rhythm: Swing
Tempo: ♩ = 132

All of me, _____ why not take all of me? _____

Can't you see _____ I'm no good with - out you? _____

Take my lips, _____ I want to lose them, _____

take my arms _____ I'll ne - ver use them.

Francis Day & Hunter Ltd, London WC2H 0EA

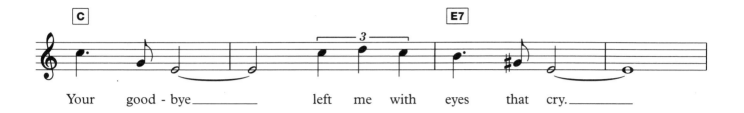

Your good-bye_____ left me with eyes that cry._____

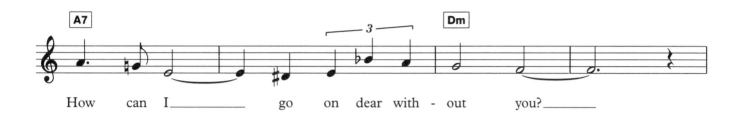

How can I_____ go on dear with - out you?_____

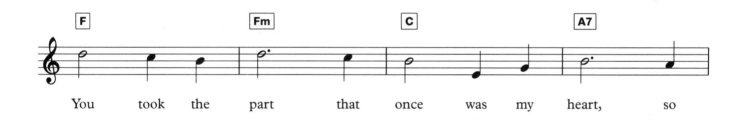

You took the part that once was my heart, so

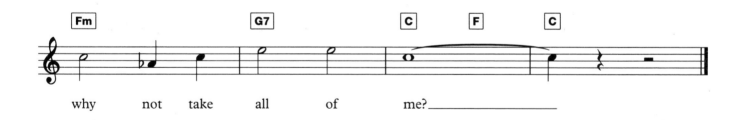

why not take all of me?_____

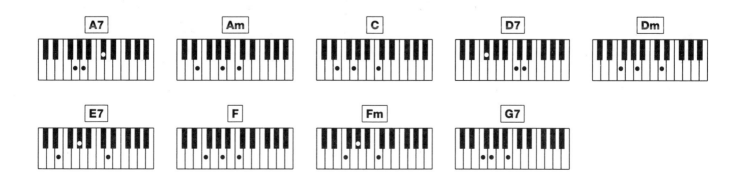

Body And Soul

Words by Robert Sour, Edward Heyman and Frank Eyton / Music by Johnny Green

Suggested Registration: Vibraphone
Rhythm: Slow Swing
Tempo: ♩ = 80

My heart is sad and lone - ly, for you I cry, for you dear on - ly.

I tell you, I mean it, I'm all for you bo - dy and soul.

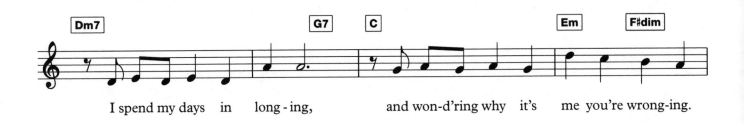

I spend my days in long - ing, and won-d'ring why it's me you're wrong-ing.

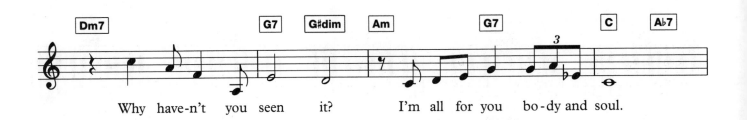

Why have-n't you seen it? I'm all for you bo - dy and soul.

I can't be-lieve it, it's hard to con-ceive it, that you'd turn a - way ro - mance.

Are you pre-tend-ing? Don't say it's the end-ing. I wish I could have one more

chance to prove, dear, my life a hell you're mak - ing. You know I'm yours for

just the tak-ing, I'd glad-ly sur - ren - der my-self to you bo-dy and soul.

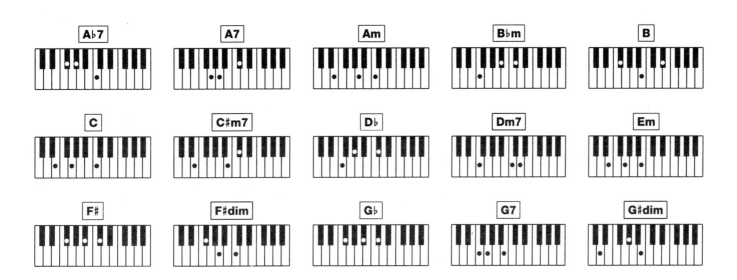

Easy To Love

Words and Music by Cole Porter

Suggested Registration: Electric Piano
Rhythm: Slow Swing
Tempo: ♩ = 104

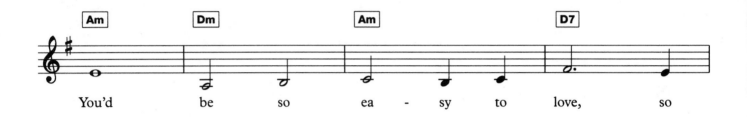

You'd be so ea - sy to love, so

ea - sy to i - do - lize all oth - ers a - bove,

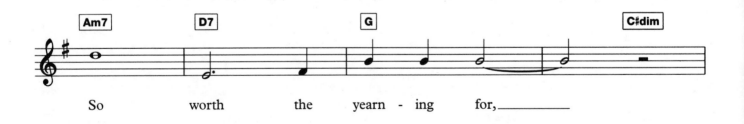

So worth the yearn - ing for,_____

so swell to keep ev - ery home - fire burn - ing for._____

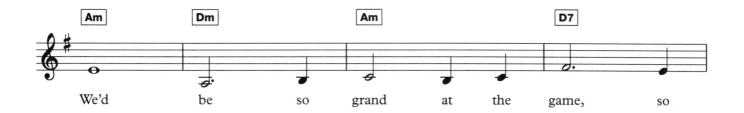

We'd be so grand at the game, so

care - free to - ge - ther, that it does seem a shame that

you can't see your fu - ture with me, 'cause you'd be

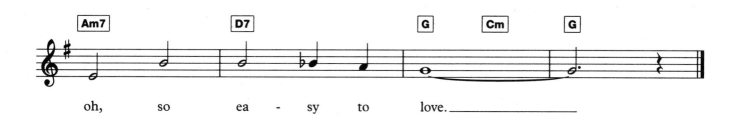

oh, so ea - sy to love. _____

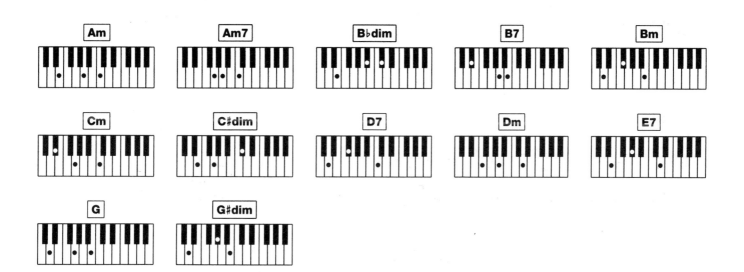

EXACTLY LIKE YOU

Words by Dorothy Fields / Music by Jimmy McHugh

Suggested Registration: Strings
Rhythm: Swing
Tempo: ♩ = 136

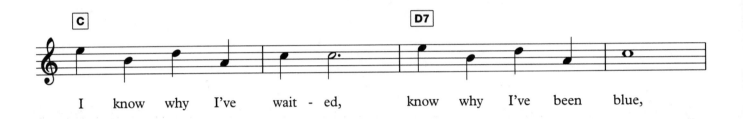

I know why I've wait - ed, know why I've been blue,

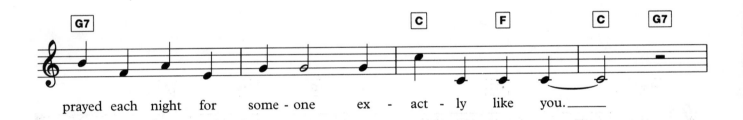

prayed each night for some - one ex - act - ly like you.____

Why should we spend mon - ey on a show or two?

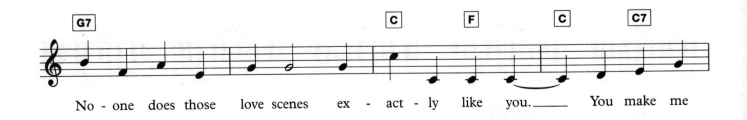

No - one does those love scenes ex - act - ly like you.____ You make me

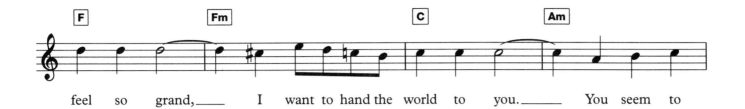

feel so grand,_____ I want to hand the world to you._____ You seem to

un - der - stand_____ each fool-ish lit - tle scheme I'm schem-ing, dream I'm dream-ing.

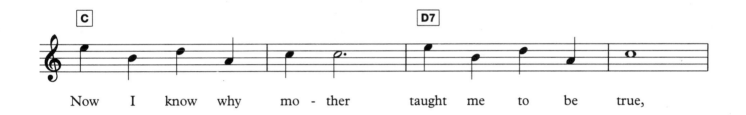

Now I know why mo - ther taught me to be true,

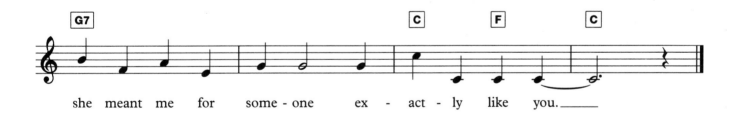

she meant me for some - one ex - act - ly like you._____

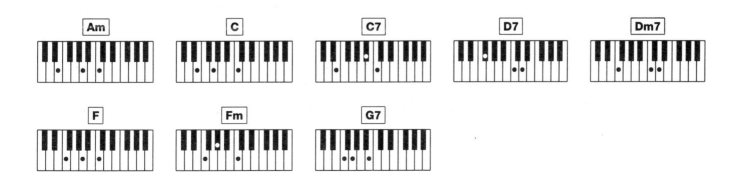

A Fine Romance

Words by Dorothy Fields / Music by Jerome Kern

Suggested Registration: Vibraphone
Rhythm: Swing
Tempo: ♩ = 132

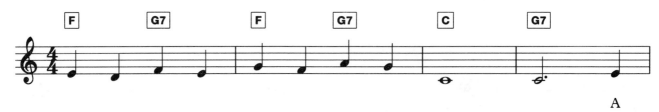

A

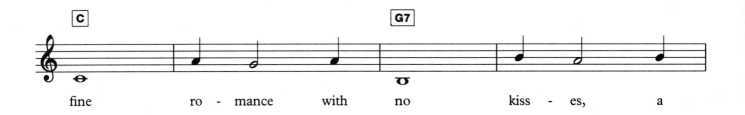

fine   ro - mance   with   no   kiss - es,   a

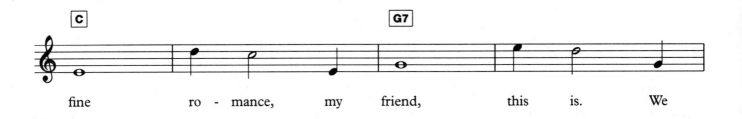

fine   ro - mance,   my   friend,   this   is.   We

should   be   like   a   cou - ple   of   hot   to - ma - toes,_____   but

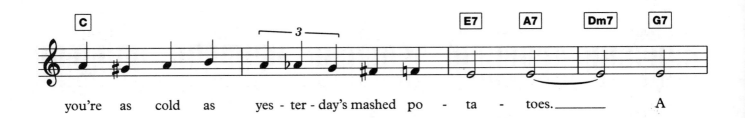

you're   as   cold   as   yes - ter - day's   mashed   po - ta - toes._____   A

fine ro - mance, you won't nes - tle, a

fine ro - mance, you won't wres - tle. I

might as well play bridge with my old maid aunts, I have - n't got a

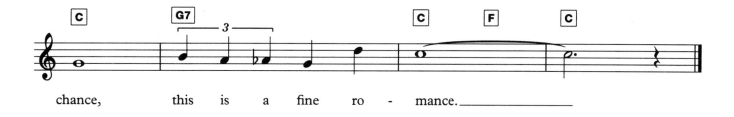

chance, this is a fine ro - mance._____

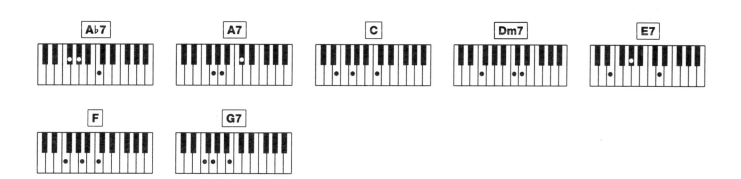

A Foggy Day

Music and Lyrics by George Gershwin and Ira Gershwin

Suggested Registration: Strings
Rhythm: Swing
Tempo: ♩ = 118

- dered, could this thing last?_____ But the age of mi -

- ra - cles had - n't passed,_____ for sud - den - ly_____

_ I saw you there,_____ and through fog - gy Lon - don

town the sun was shin - ing ev - ery - where._____

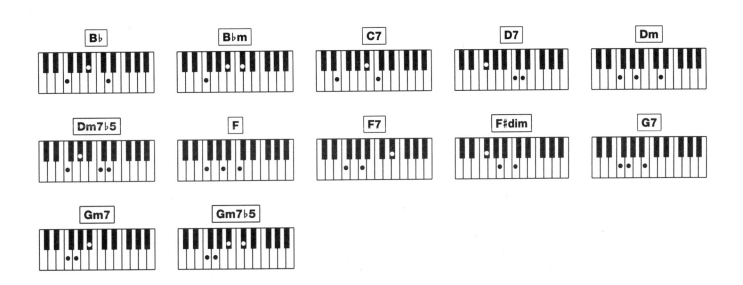

For All We Know

Words by Sam M Lewis / Music by J Fred Coots

Suggested Registration: Strings
Rhythm: Slow Swing
Tempo: ♩ = 94

For all we know, we may ne - ver meet a - gain,

be - fore you go, make this mo-ment sweet a - gain.

We won't say 'Good - night,' un - til the last

min - ute, I'll hold out my hand, and my heart will be

Warner Bros Publications Inc / IMP Ltd and Redwood Music Ltd, London NW1 8BD

in it. For all we know, this may on - ly be a dream,__

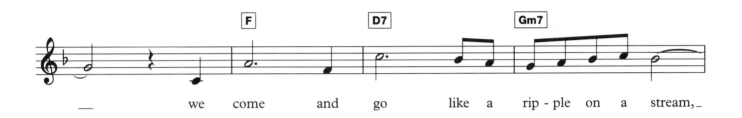

__ we come and go like a rip - ple on a stream,__

__ so love me to - night, to - mor - row was made for

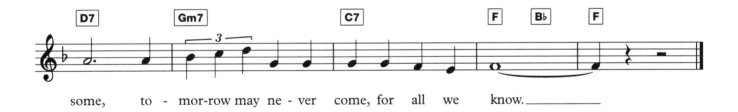

some, to - mor-row may ne - ver come, for all we know._____

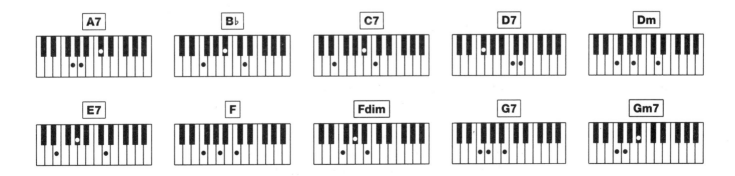

GLORY OF LOVE

Words and Music by Billy Hill

Suggested Registration: Vibraphone
Rhythm: Swing
Tempo: ♩ = 126

You've got to

give a lit-tle, take a lit-tle, and let your poor heart break a lit-tle,

that's the sto-ry of, that's the glo-ry of love._____ You've got to

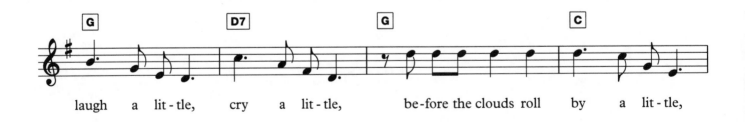

laugh a lit-tle, cry a lit-tle, be-fore the clouds roll by a lit-tle,

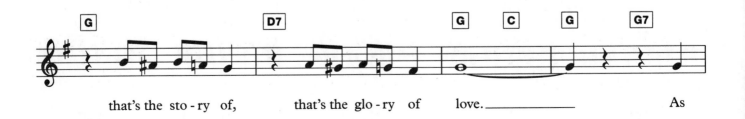

that's the sto-ry of, that's the glo-ry of love._____ As

long as there's the two of us, we've got the world and all its charms, and

when the world is through with us, we've got each oth - er's arms. You've got to

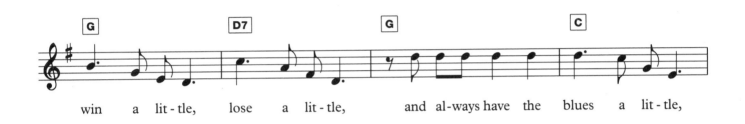

win a lit - tle, lose a lit - tle, and al-ways have the blues a lit - tle,

that's the sto - ry of, that's the glo - ry of love._____

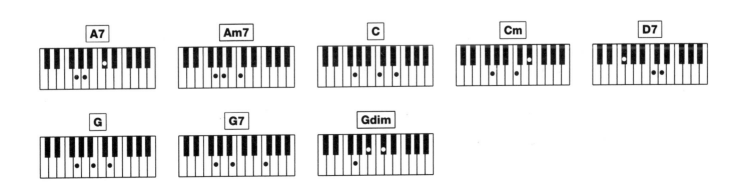

I Wanna Be Loved By You

Words by Bert Kalmar / Music by Herbert Stothart and Harry Ruby

Suggested Registration: Saxophone
Rhythm: Swing
Tempo: ♩ = 112

I wan-na be loved by you, just you, and no-bo-dy else but you,

I wan-na be loved by you a - lone,_____ poo-poo - pa-doop.

I wan-na be kissed by you, just you, and no-bo-dy else but you,

I wan-na be kissed by you a - lone, poo-poo - pa-doop. I could-n't as -

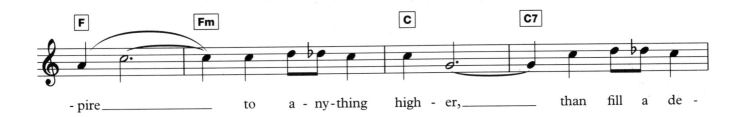

-pire _____ to a - ny-thing high - er,_____ than fill a de -

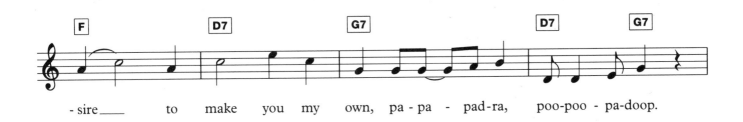

- sire ____ to make you my own, pa - pa - pad-ra, poo-poo - pa-doop.

I wan-na be loved by you, just you, and no - bo - dy else but you,

I wan-na be loved by you a - lone, pa-dap-pa dap-pa-dab, po-poo - pa-doop.

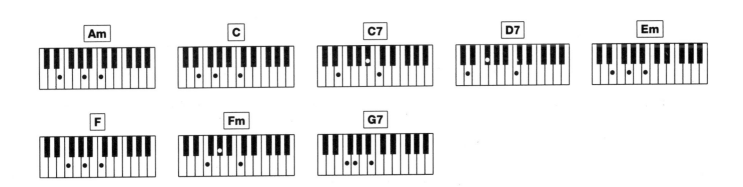

I'VE GOT YOU UNDER MY SKIN

Words and Music by Cole Porter

Suggested Registration: Vibraphone 205 -038
Rhythm: Swing
Tempo: ♩ = 106

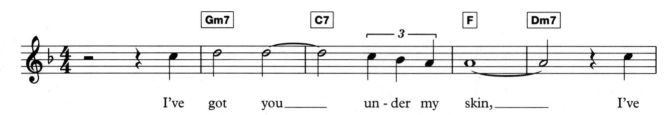

I've got you _____ un-der my skin, _____ I've

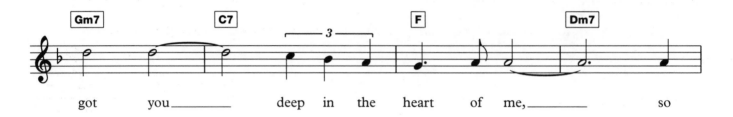

got you _____ deep in the heart of me, _____ so

deep in my heart _____ you're real-ly a part of me, _____ I've

got you _____ un-der my skin. _____ I'll

sac-ri-fice a-ny-thing, come what might, for the sake of hav-ing you

near, in spite of the warn-ing voice that comes in the night, and re-

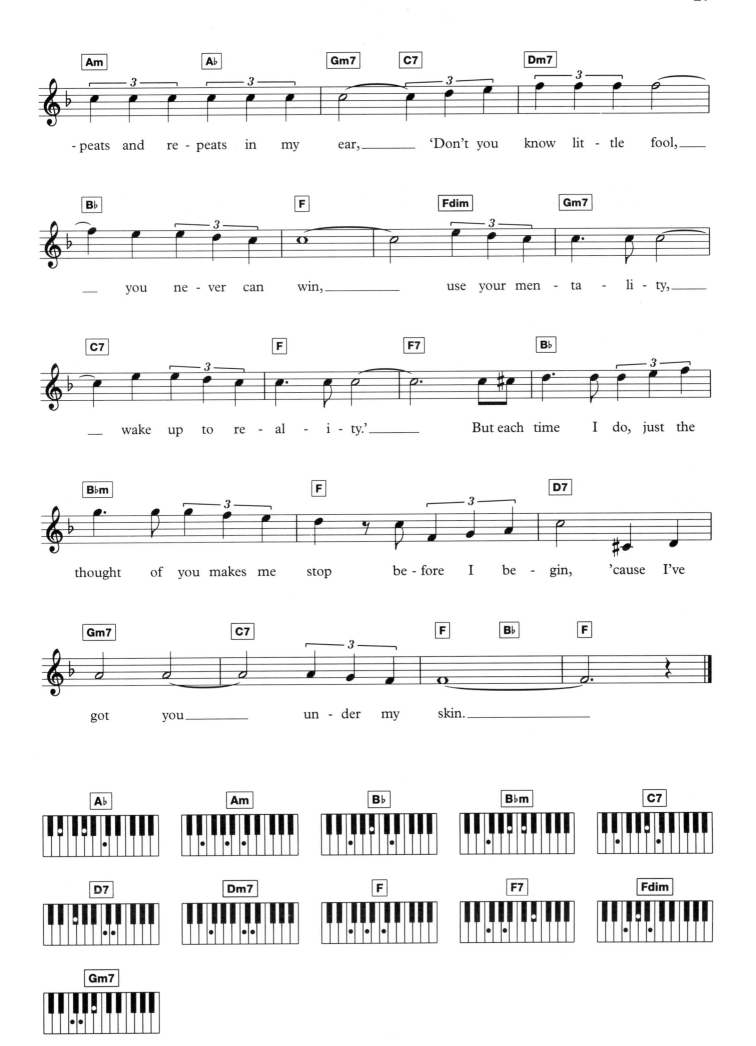

KEEP YOUNG AND BEAUTIFUL

Words by Al Dubin / Music by Harry Warren

Suggested Registration: Vibraphone
Rhythm: Swing
Tempo: ♩ = 130

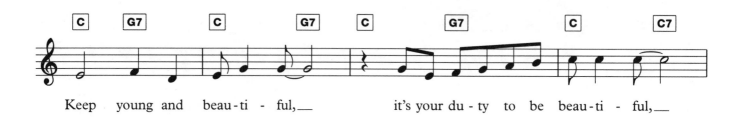

Keep young and beau-ti - ful,___ it's your du - ty to be beau-ti - ful,___

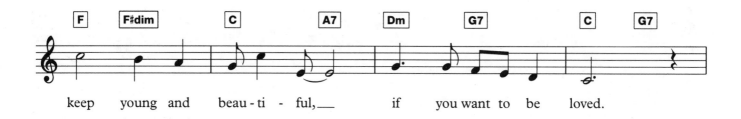

keep young and beau-ti - ful,___ if you want to be loved.

Don't fail to do your stuff, with a lit - tle pow-der and a puff,___

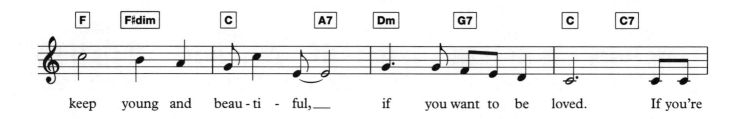

keep young and beau-ti - ful,___ if you want to be loved. If you're

wise, ex - er - cise all the fat off, take it off, off - a here, off - a there. When you're

seen a - ny-where with your hat off, have a Mar - cel wave in your hair.

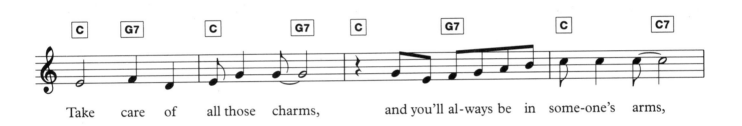

Take care of all those charms, and you'll al-ways be in some-one's arms,

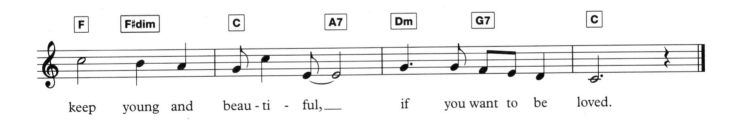

keep young and beau - ti - ful,___ if you want to be loved.

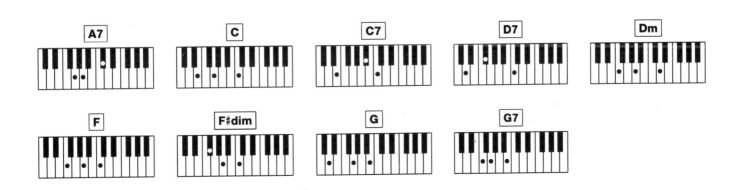

The Lady Is A Tramp

Words by Lorenz Hart / Music by Richard Rodgers

Suggested Registration: Saxophone
Rhythm: Swing
Tempo: ♩ = 132

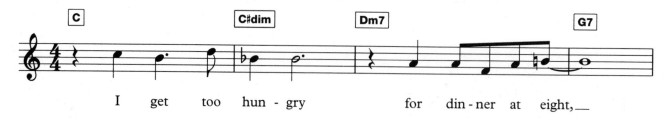

I get too hun-gry for din-ner at eight,___

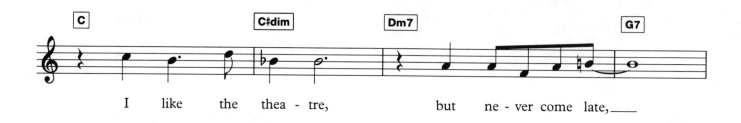

I like the thea-tre, but ne-ver come late,___

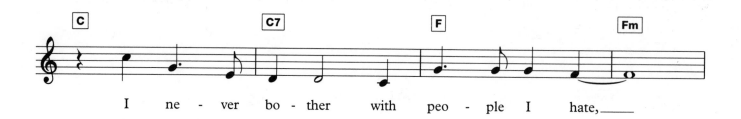

I ne-ver bo-ther with peo-ple I hate,____

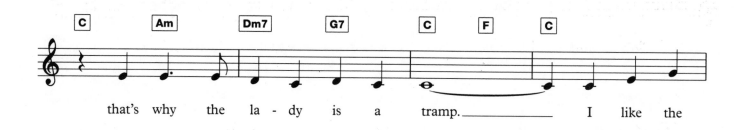

that's why the la-dy is a tramp._____ I like the

free, fresh wind in my hair,_____

life with-out care, ___ I'm broke, it's oke,

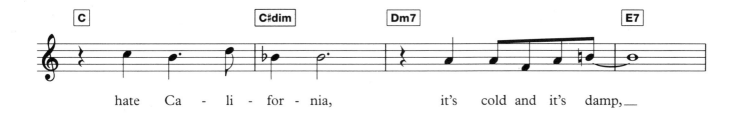

hate Ca - li - for - nia, it's cold and it's damp, __

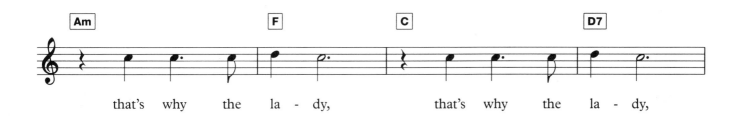

that's why the la - dy, that's why the la - dy,

that's why the la - dy is a tramp. _____

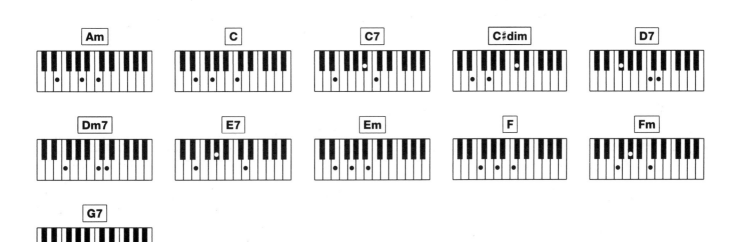

Lazy Bones

Words and Music by Johnny Mercer and Hoagy Carmichael
Additional Lyrics by Horatio Nicholls

Suggested Registration: Vibraphone
Rhythm: Slow Swing
Tempo: ♩ = 72

La - zy bones, sleep - in' in the sun, how you 'spec' to get your

day's work done? Ne - ver get your day's work done,

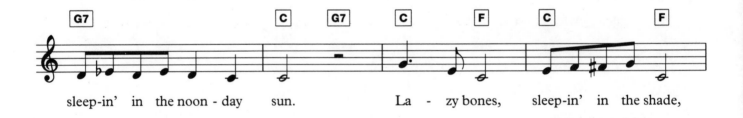

sleep - in' in the noon - day sun. La - zy bones, sleep - in' in the shade,

how you 'spec' to get your corn - meal made? Ne - ver get your corn - meal made,

sleep - in' in the eve - nin' shade. When 'ta - ters needs spray - in', I

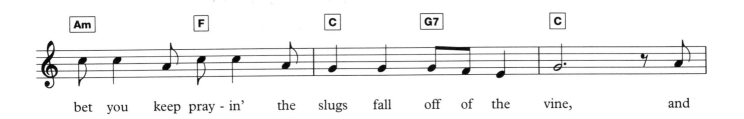

bet you keep pray - in' the slugs fall off of the vine, and

when you go fish-in', I bet you keep wish-in' the fish won't grab at your line.

La - zy bones, loaf-in' through the day, how you 'spec' to make a dime that way?

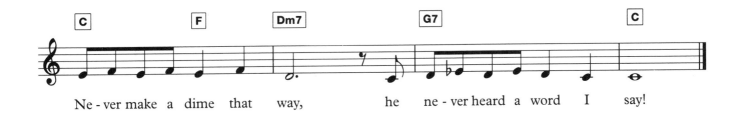

Ne - ver make a dime that way, he ne - ver heard a word I say!

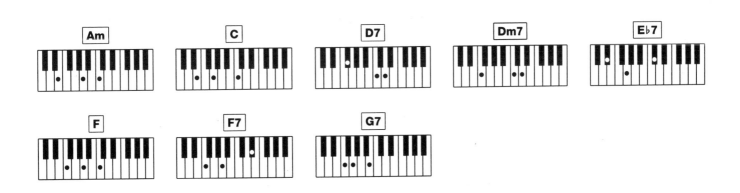

MOONLIGHT SERENADE

Words by Mitchell Parish / Music by Glenn Miller

Suggested Registration: Saxophone
Rhythm: Slow Swing
Tempo: ♩ = 72

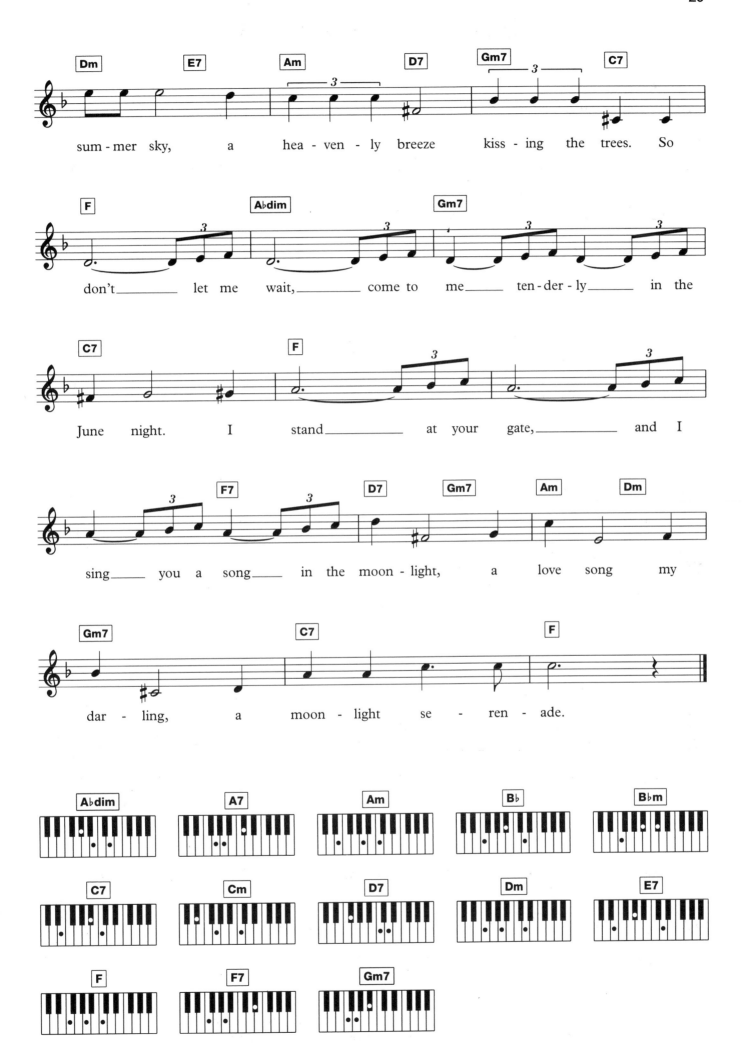

Over The Rainbow

Words by E Y Harburg / Music by Harold Arlen

Suggested Registration: Flute
Rhythm: Soft Rock
Tempo: ♩ = 82

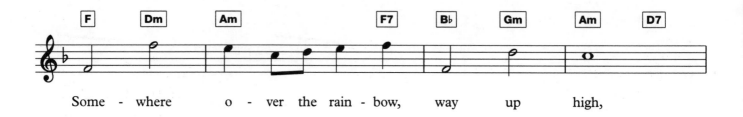

Some - where   o - ver the rain - bow,   way   up   high,

there's   a   land that I heard of   once   in a lul - la - by.

Some - where   o - ver the rain - bow,   skies   are   blue,

and   the   dreams that you dare to   dream real - ly do come   true.   Some

day I'll wish up-on a star, and wake up where the clouds are far be-hind me.____

____ Where trou-bles melt like le-mon drops a - way a-bove the chim-ney tops, that's

where you'll find me. Some-where o - ver the rain-bow, blue - birds fly,

birds fly o - ver the rain-bow, why then, oh why can't I?

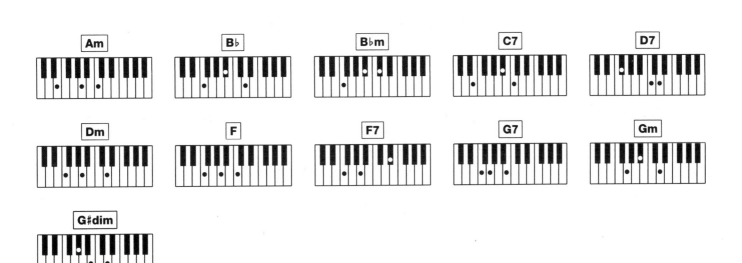

SMOKE GETS IN YOUR EYES

Words by Otto Harbach / Music by Jerome Kern

Suggested Registration: Acoustic Guitar
Rhythm: Soft Rock
Tempo: ♩ = 72

They asked me how I knew my true love was true,_____

—— I, of course, re - plied, 'Some-thing here in - side can - not be de-

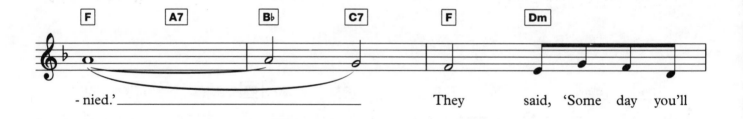

- nied.'_____ They said, 'Some day you'll

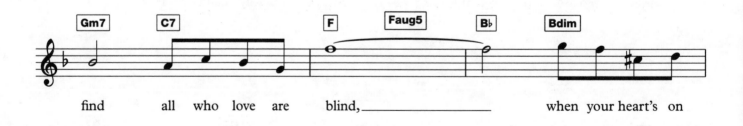

find all who love are blind,_____ when your heart's on

fire, you must re - a - lize, smoke gets in your eyes.'_____

PolyGram Music Publishing Ltd, London W6 9XT

33

So I chaffed them and I gai - ly laughed to think they could doubt my love.

Yet to - day,___ my love has flown a - way,___ I am with - out my love.

Now, laugh-ing friends de - ride tears I can-not hide,_____ so I smile and

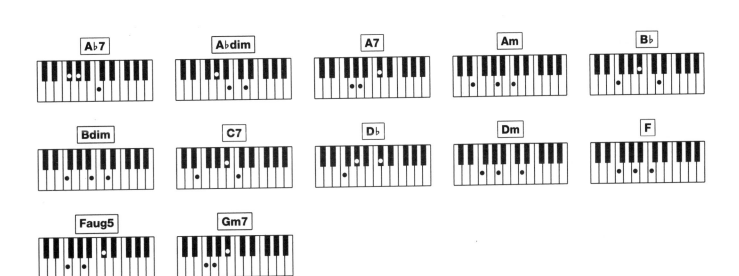

say, 'When a love-ly flame dies, smoke gets in your eyes.'_____

Stormy Weather

Words by Ted Koehler / Music by Harold Arlen

Suggested Registration: Vibraphone
Rhythm: Slow Swing
Tempo: ♩ = 78

Don't know why there's no sun up in the sky, stor-my wea-ther,_

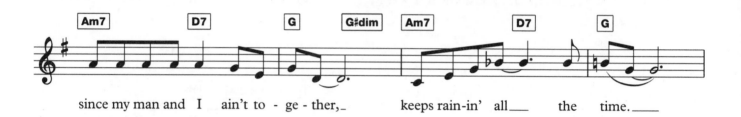

since my man and I ain't to - ge - ther,_ keeps rain-in' all__ the time.___

Life is bare, gloom and mis-'ry ev - ery-where, stor-my wea-ther,_

just can't get my poor self to - ge - ther,_ I'm wea-ry all__ the time,___ the

time,___ so wea-ry all__ the time.___ When he went a - way the blues walked

in and met me,___ if he stays a-way, old rock-in' chair will get me.___

All I do is pray the Lord a-bove will let me___ walk in the sun once more. Can't go

on, ev-ery-thing I had is gone, stor-my wea-ther,_ since my man and I ain't to-

-ge-ther,___ keeps rain-in' all____ the time,_____

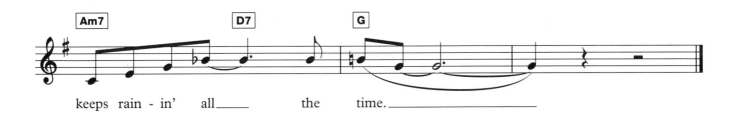

keeps rain-in' all____ the time._____

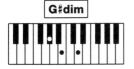

SUMMERTIME

By George Gershwin, Dubose Heyward, Dorothy Heyward and Ira Gershwin

Suggested Registration: Harmonica
Rhythm: Slow Swing
Tempo: ♩ = 74

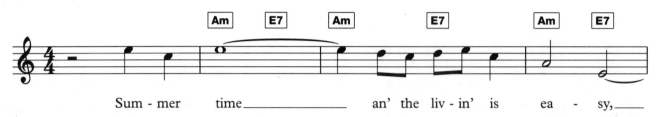

Sum - mer time _____ an' the liv - in' is ea - sy, _____

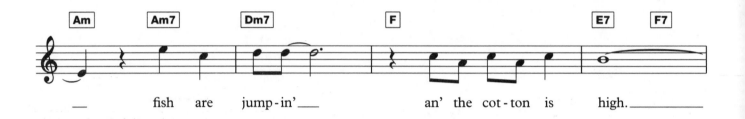

___ fish are jump - in' ___ an' the cot - ton is high. _____

___ Oh, yo' dad - dy's rich, ___ an' yo' ma is good look - in', ___

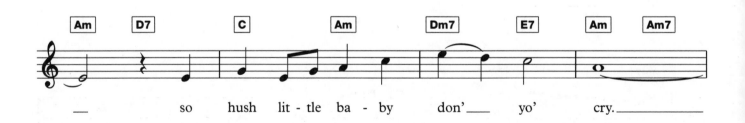

___ so hush lit - tle ba - by don' ___ yo' cry. _____

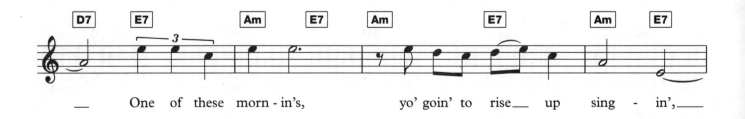

___ One of these morn - in's, yo' goin' to rise ___ up sing - in',

Walkin' My Baby Back Home

Words and Music by Roy Turk and Fred E Ahlert

Suggested Registration: Saxophone *143*
Rhythm: Swing *048 - 049*
Tempo: ♩ = 100

Gee, it's great_ af-ter be-in' out late,_ walk-in' my ba - by back home,

arm in arm_ o-ver mea-dow and farm, walk-in' my ba - by back home.

We go 'long_ har-mon-iz-in' a song, or I'm re-cit - ing a poem,

owls go by __ and they give me the eye, _ walk-in' my ba - by back home. We

stop for a while, she gives me a smile, and snug-gles her head to my chest. We

start in to pet,_ and that's when I get_ her pow - der all o - ver my vest._

Af - ter I___ kind - a straight-en my tie,___ she has to bor - row my comb,

one kiss then, I con - tin - ue a - gain,_ walk-in' my ba - by back home.

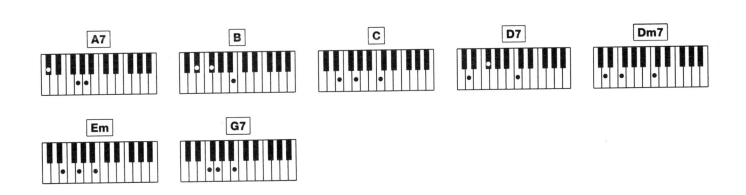

The Way You Look Tonight

Words by Dorothy Fields / Music by Jerome Kern

Suggested Registration: Strings
Rhythm: Soft Rock
Tempo: ♩ = 72

Some day, when I'm aw - f'ly low, when the world is cold,

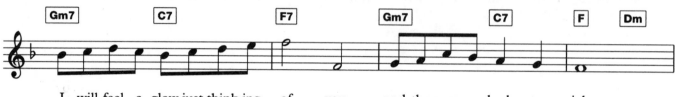

I will feel a glow just think-ing of you, and the way you look to - night.

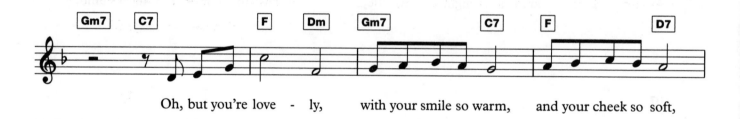

Oh, but you're love - ly, with your smile so warm, and your cheek so soft,

there is no-thing for me but to love you, just the way you look to - night.

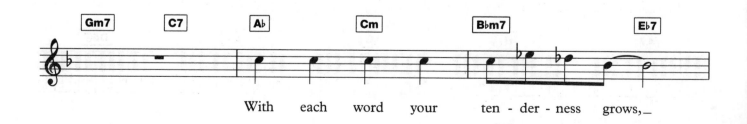

With each word your ten - der - ness grows,__

tear - ing my fear____ a - part, and that laugh that

wrin-kles your nose,__ touch-es my fool - ish heart. Love - ly,

ne - ver, ne - ver change, keep that breath-less charm. Won't you please ar-range it? 'Cause I

love you, just the way you look to - night._____

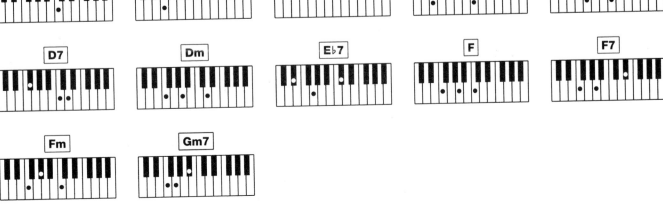

What A Difference A Day Made

Music and Spanish Words by Maria Grever / English Words by Stanley Adams

Suggested Registration: Acoustic Guitar
Rhythm: Rhumba / Latin
Tempo: ♩ = 124

What a dif-f'rence a day made,____ twen-ty-four lit-tle ho-urs,____

____ brought the sun and the flo-wers____ where there used to be rain.____

____ My yes-ter-day was blue, dear,____ to-day, I'm part of you dear,__

__ my lone-ly nights are through, dear,____ since you said you were mine.____

Gm7   C7   F

___ What a dif-f'rence a day makes,___ there's a rain-bow be - fore me,___

Gm7   C7   F

___ skies a-bove can't be stor - my,___ since that mo-ment of bliss, that thrill-ing

F7   B♭   B♭m   F

kiss, it's hea-ven when you____ find ro-mance on your me - nu.____

Fdim   Gm7   C7   F

___ What a dif-f'rence a day made, and the dif-f'rence is you._____

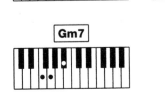

WHEN YOUR OLD WEDDING RING WAS NEW

Words by Charles McCarthy and Joe Solieri / Music by Bert Douglas

Suggested Registration: Clarinet *143*
Rhythm: Swing *048*
Tempo: ♩ = 120

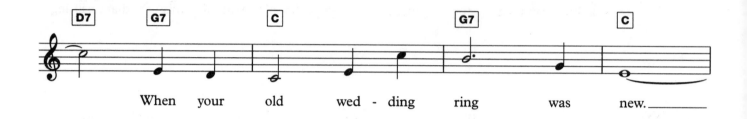

When your old wed - ding ring was new._____

_ and each dream that we dreamed came true,_____

_ I re - mem - ber with pride_____ how we stood side by side,_

_ what a beau - ti - ful pic - ture you made as my

bride. Ev - en though sil - ver crowns your hair, ___

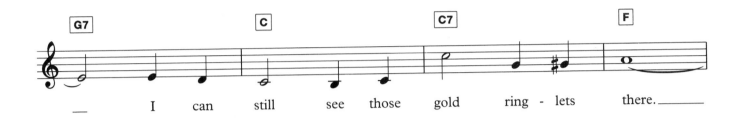

___ I can still see those gold ring - lets there. ___

___ Love's old flame is the same as the day I changed your

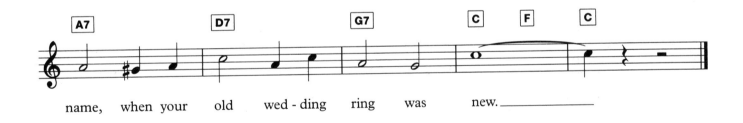

name, when your old wed - ding ring was new. ___

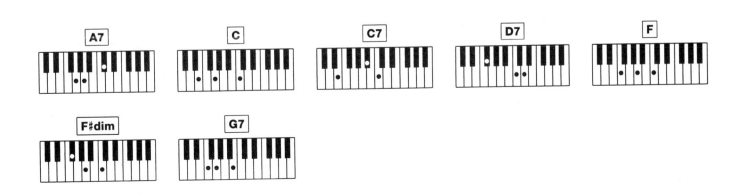

You Go To My Head

Words by Haven Gillespie / Music by J Fred Coots

Suggested Registration: Strings
Rhythm: Slow Swing
Tempo: ♩ = 90

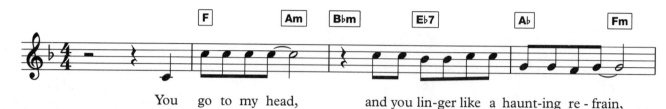

You go to my head, and you lin-ger like a haunt-ing re - frain,

and I find you spin-ning round in my brain, like the bub-bles in a glass of cham-pagne. _

— You go to my head, like a sip of spark-ling Bur-gun-dy Brew,

and I find the ve-ry men-tion of you, _ like the kick-er in a ju-lep or two. ___

— The thrill of the thought that you might give a thought to my plea casts a spell o-ver me.

— Still I say to my-self, 'Get a hold of your-self, can't you see that it ne-ver can

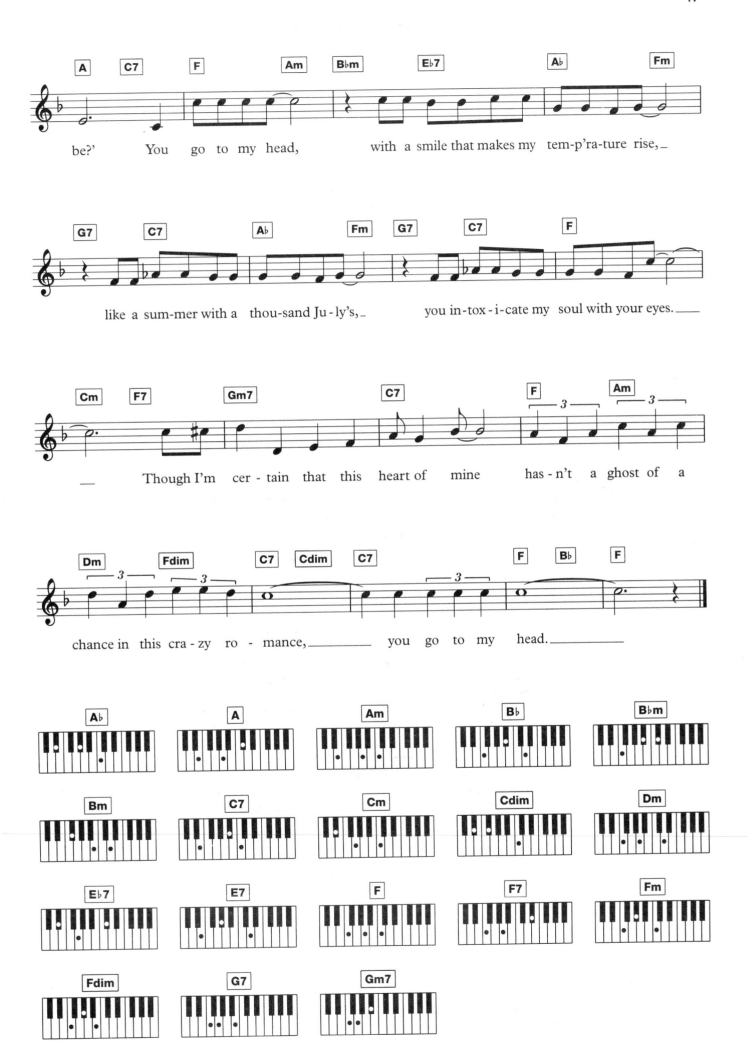

Printed by Watkiss Studios Ltd., Biggleswade, Beds. 6/95

THE EASY KEYBOARD LIBRARY

Also available in the Decades Series

THE TWENTIES
including:

Ain't Misbehavin'
Ain't She Sweet?
Baby Face
The Man I Love

My Blue Heaven
Side By Side
Spread A Little Happiness
When You're Smiling

THE THIRTIES
including:

All Of Me
A Fine Romance
I Wanna Be Loved By You
I've Got You Under My Skin

The Lady Is A Tramp
Smoke Gets In Your Eyes
Summertime
Walkin' My Baby Back Home

THE FORTIES
including:

Almost Like Being In Love
Don't Get Around Much Any More
How High The Moon
Let There Be Love

Sentimental Journey
Swinging On A Star
Tenderly
You Make Me Feel So Young

THE FIFTIES
including:

All The Way
Cry Me A River
Dream Lover
High Hopes

Magic Moments
Mister Sandman
A Teenager In Love
Whatever Will Be Will Be

THE SIXTIES
including:

Cabaret
Happy Birthday Sweet Sixteen
I'm A Believer
The Loco-motion

My Kind Of Girl
Needles And Pins
There's A Kind Of Hush
Walk On By

THE SEVENTIES
including:

Chanson D'Amour
Hi Ho Silver Lining
I'm Not In Love
Isn't She Lovely

Save Your Kisses For Me
Take Good Care Of My Baby
We've Only Just Begun
You Light Up My Life

THE EIGHTIES
including:

Anything For You
China In Your Hand
Everytime You Go Away
Golden Brown

I Want To Break Free
Karma Chameleon
Nikita
Take My Breath Away

THE NINETIES
including:

Crocodile Shoes
I Swear
A Million Love Songs
The One And Only

Promise Me
Sacrifice
Think Twice
Would I Lie To You?